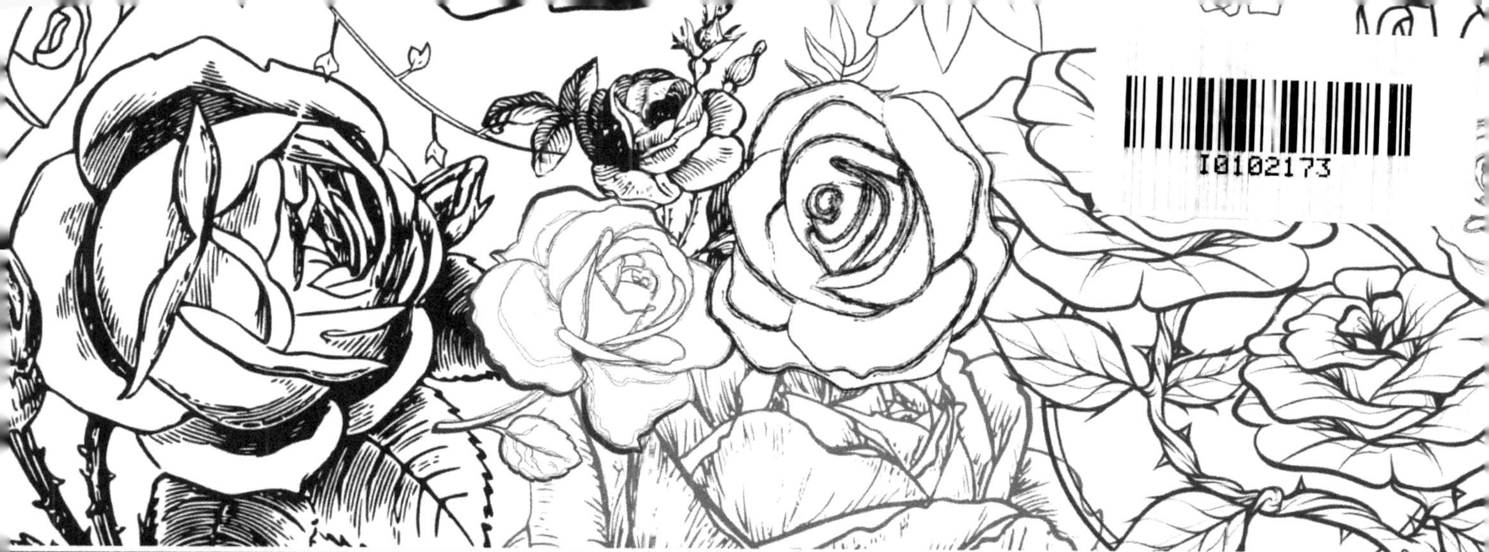



SUNSHINE SEED COLLECTION

# GARDEN ROMANCE

FLOWER COLORING BOOK

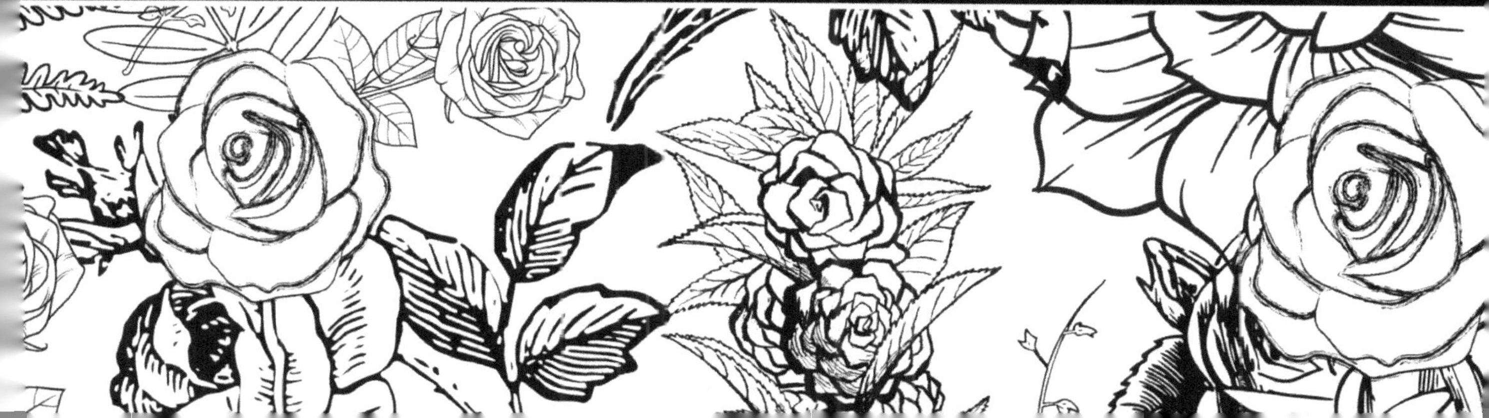

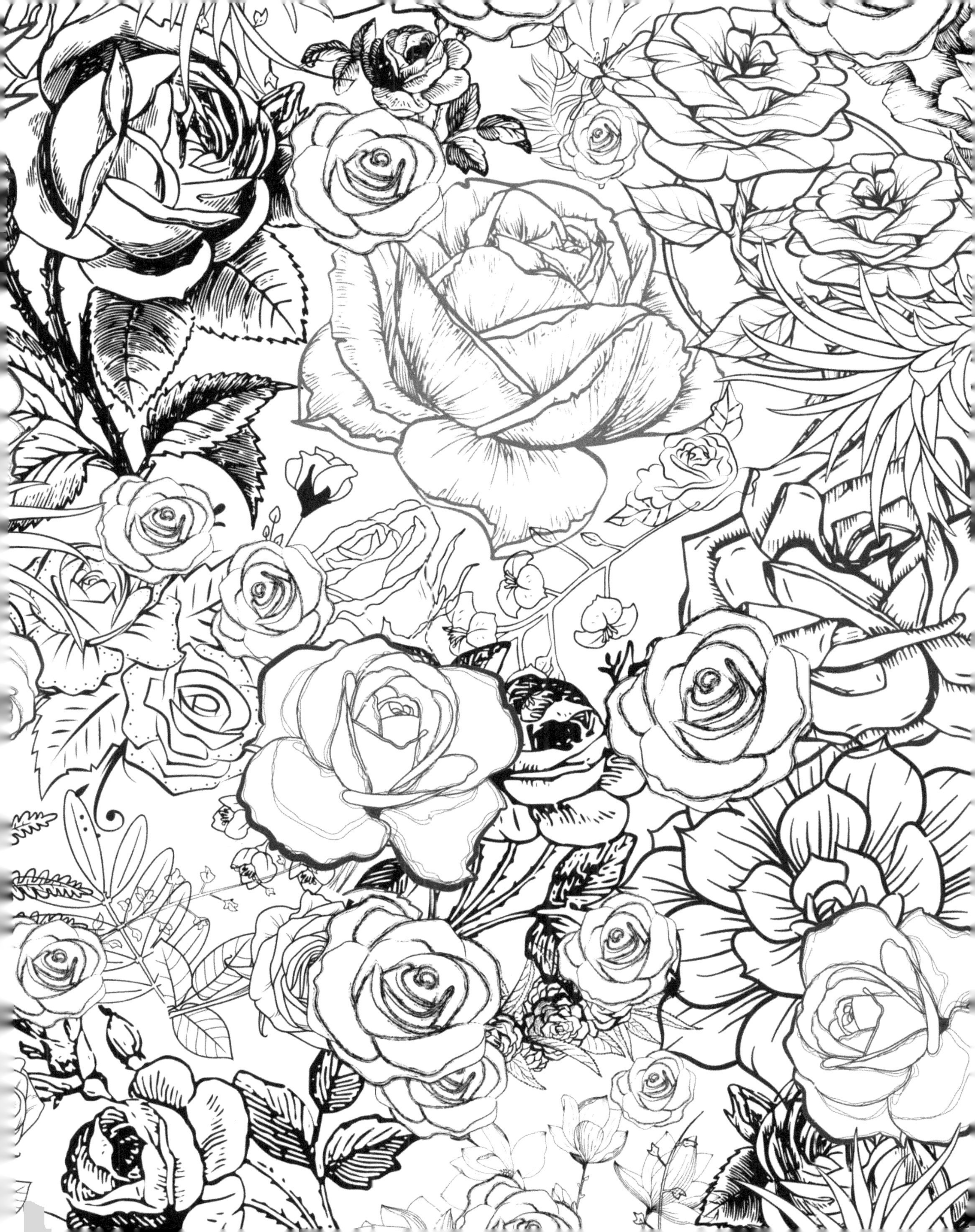

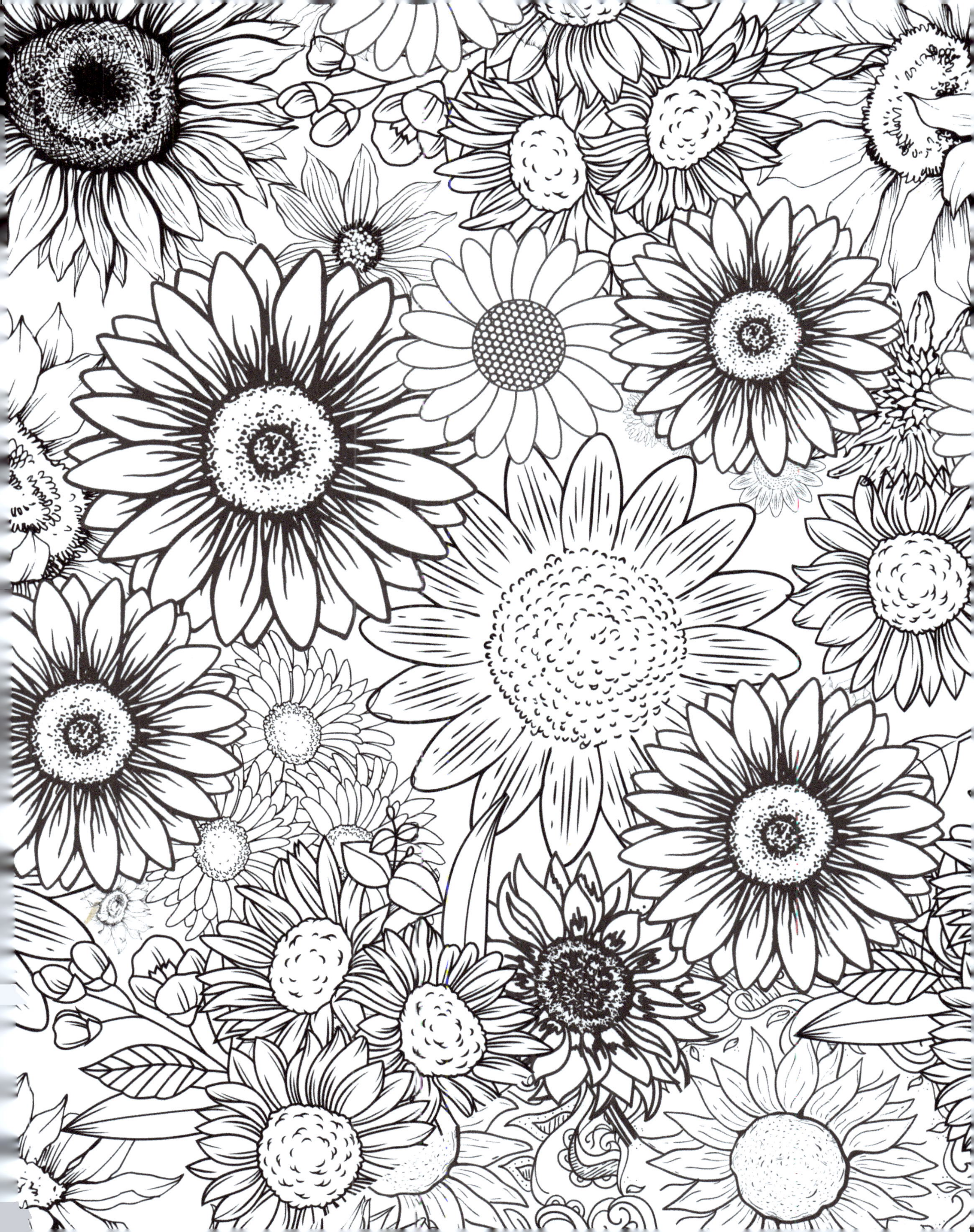

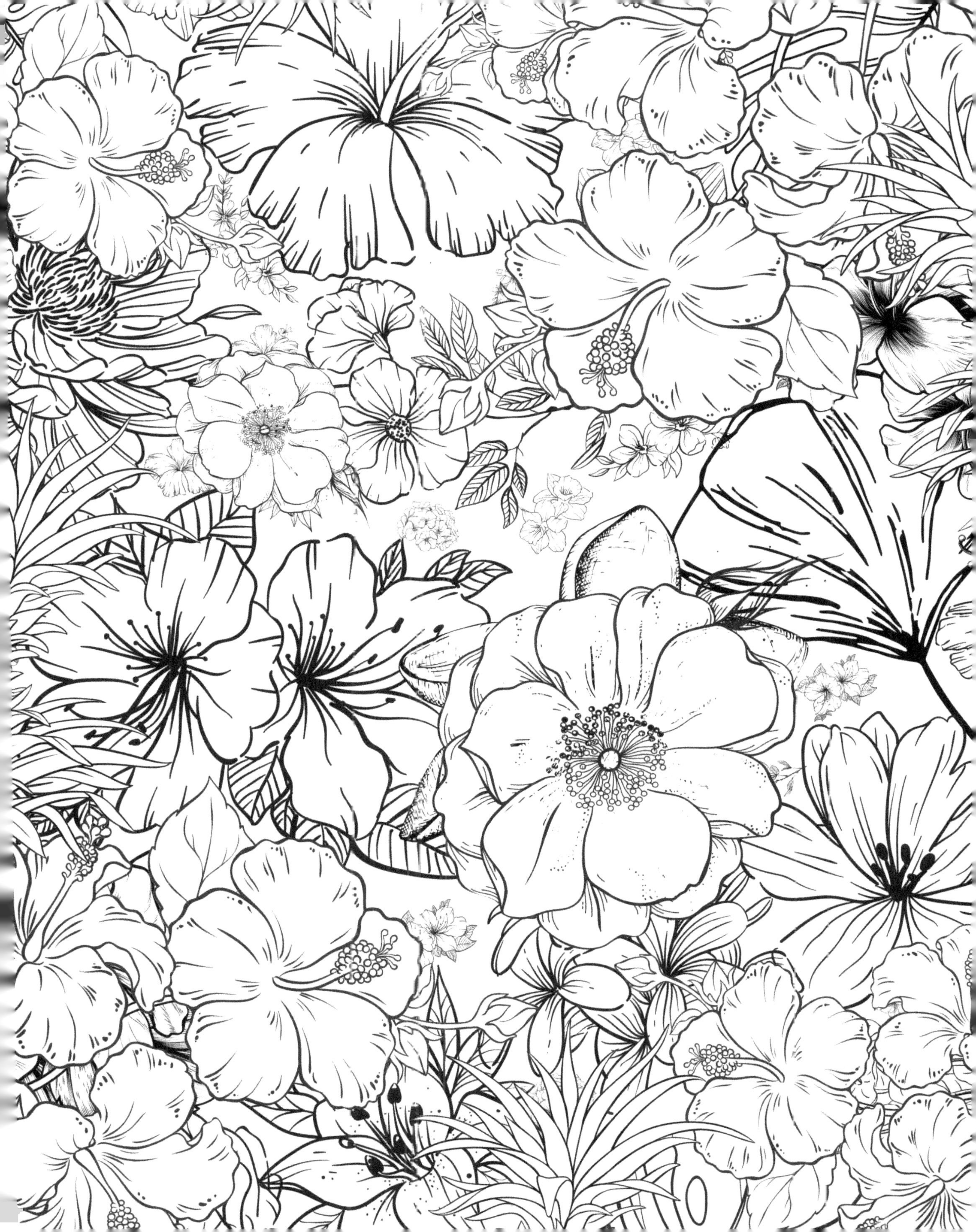

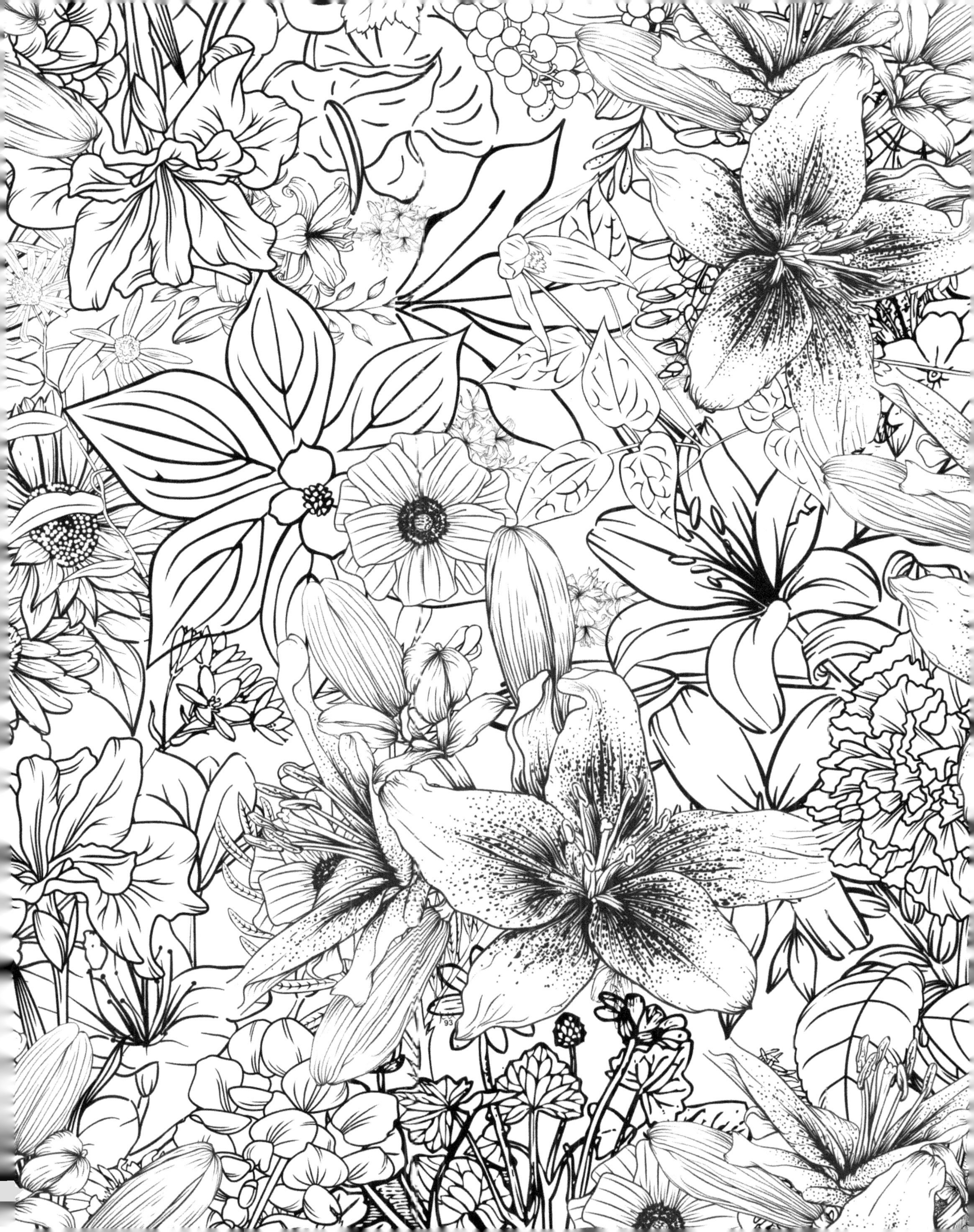

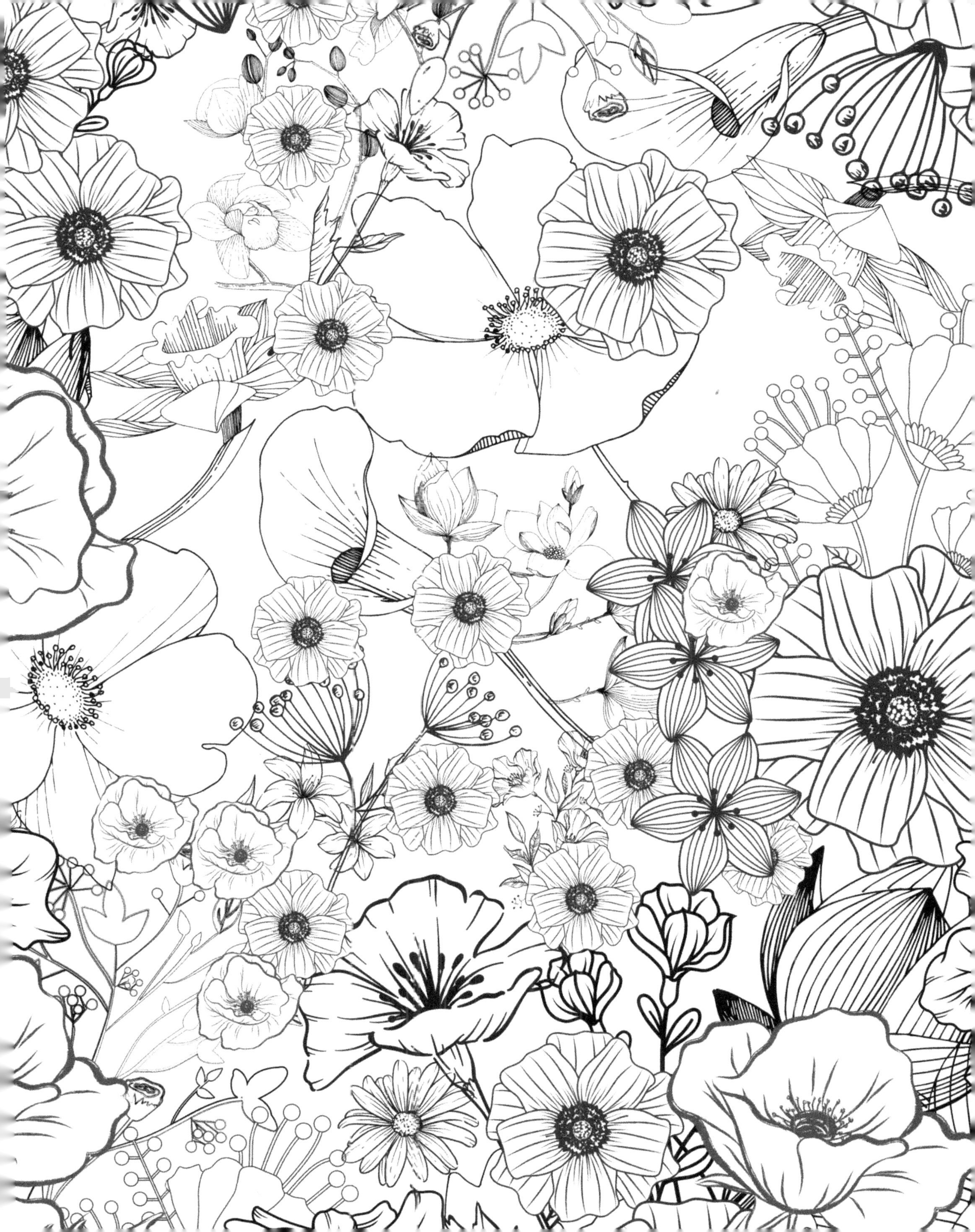

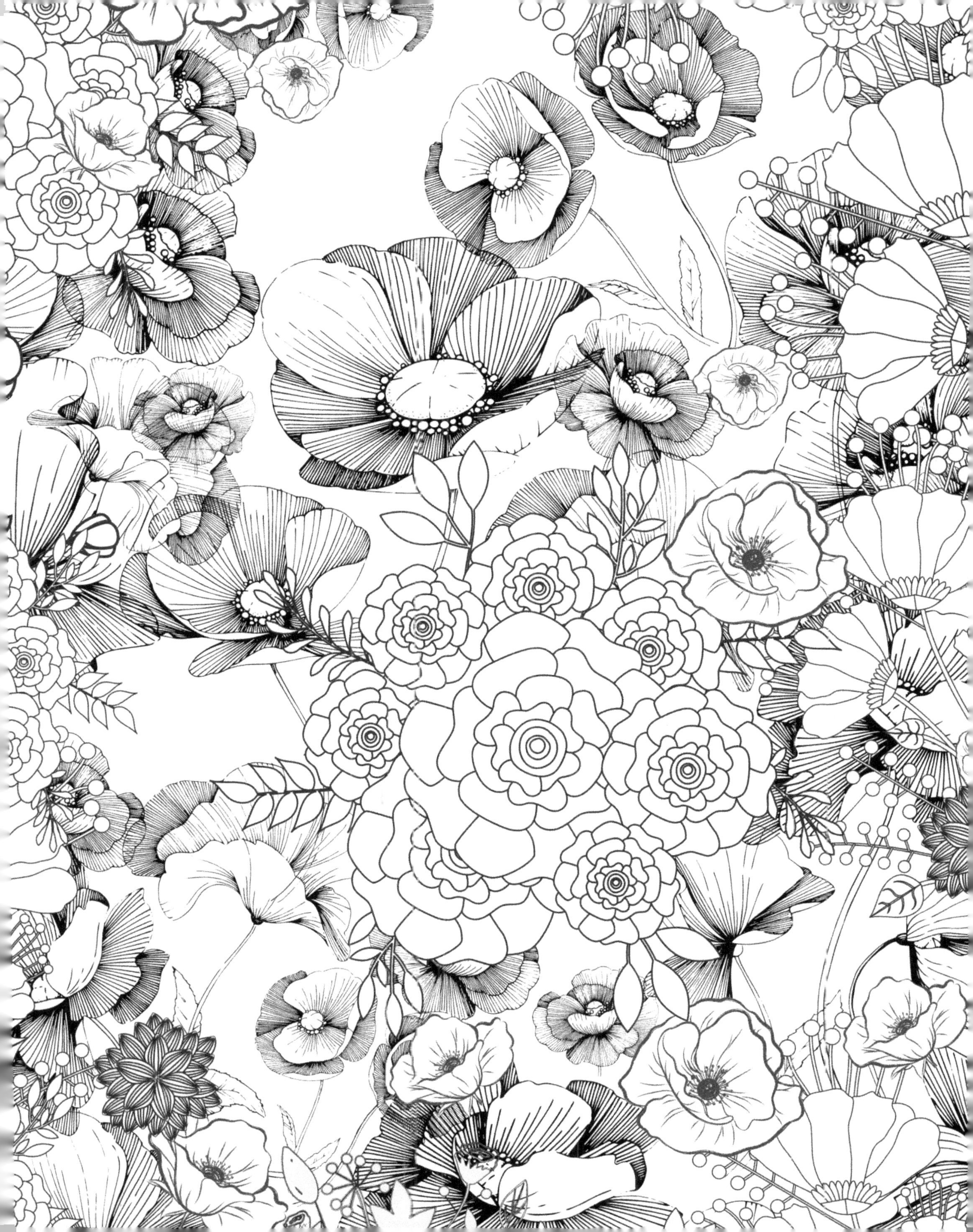

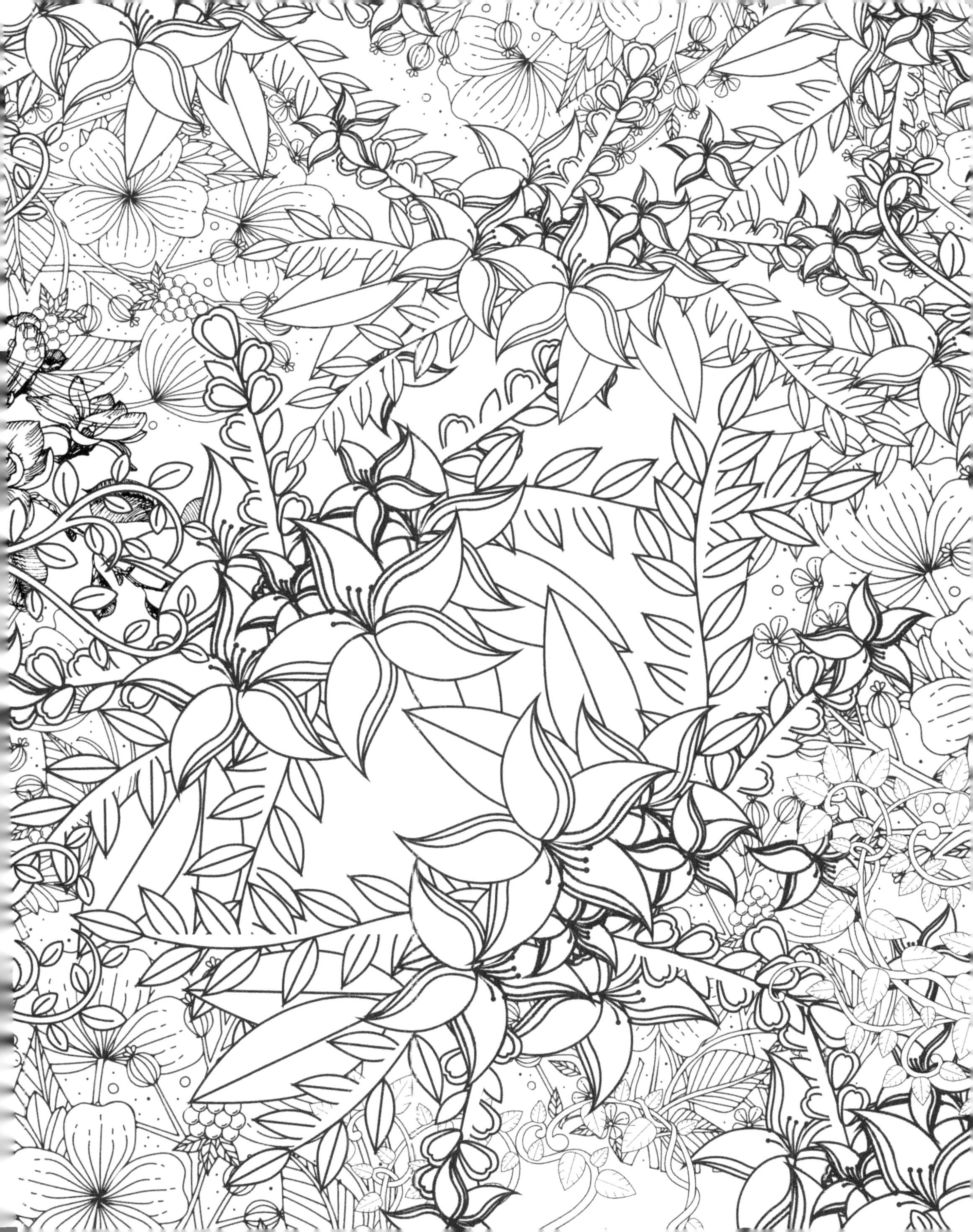

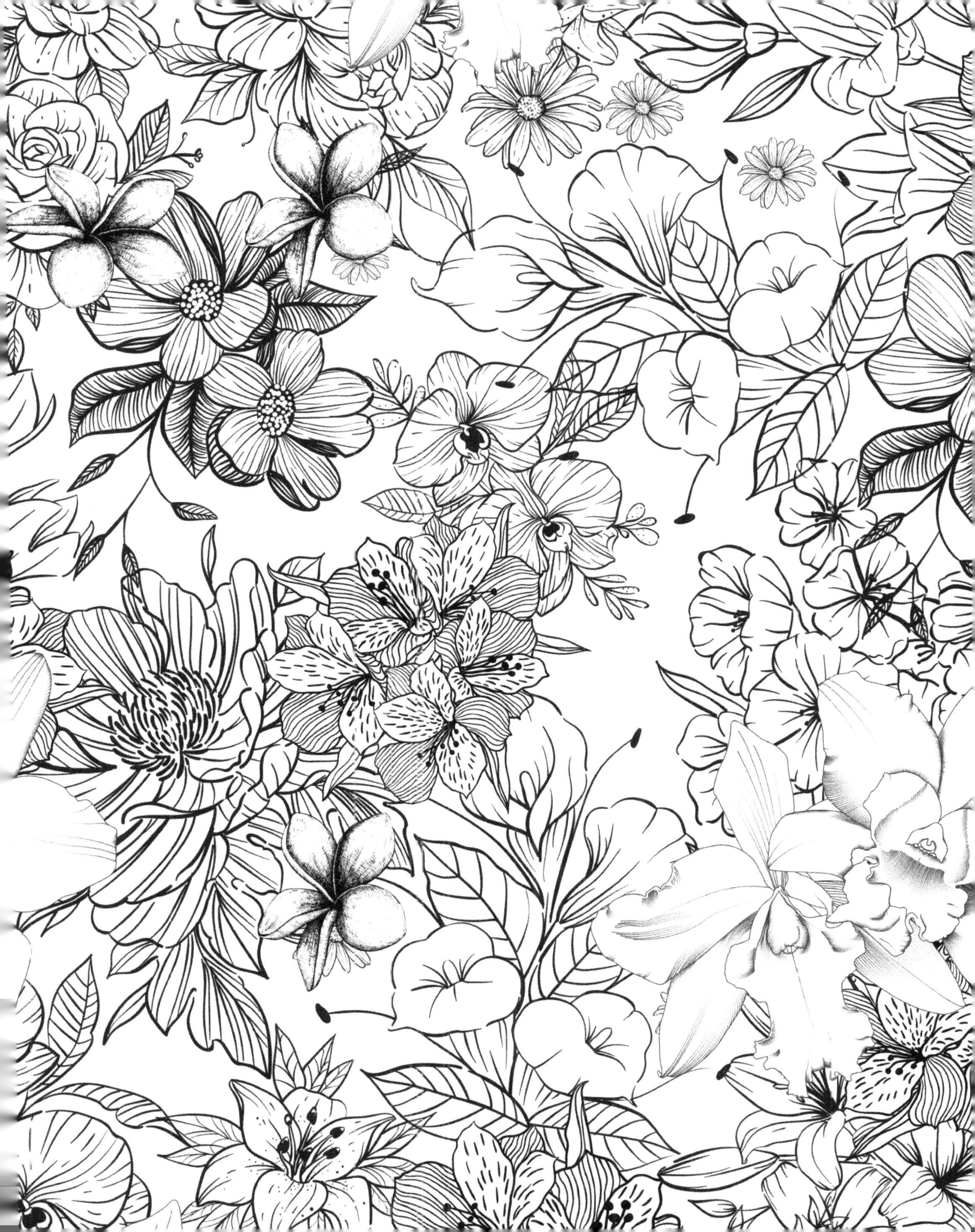

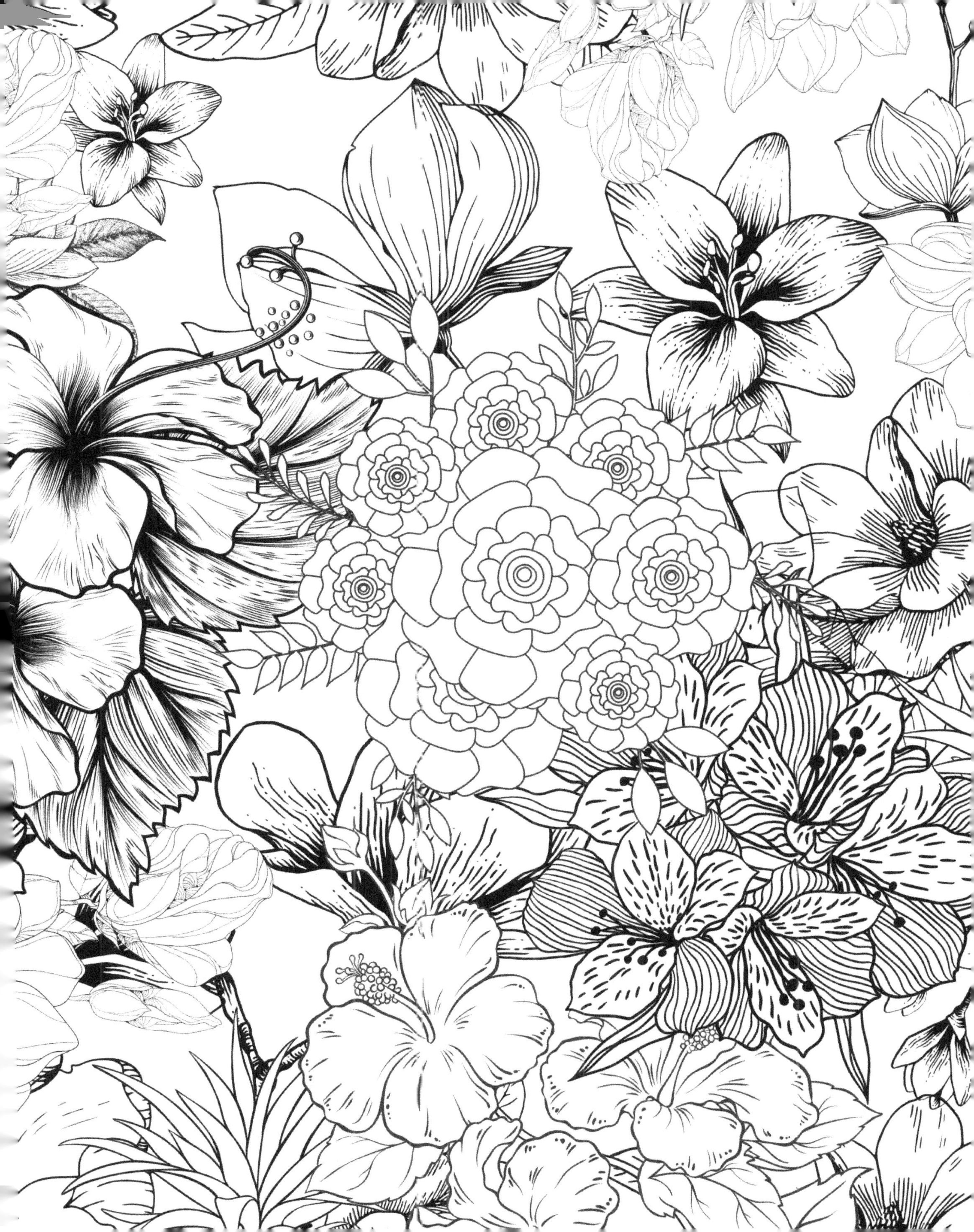

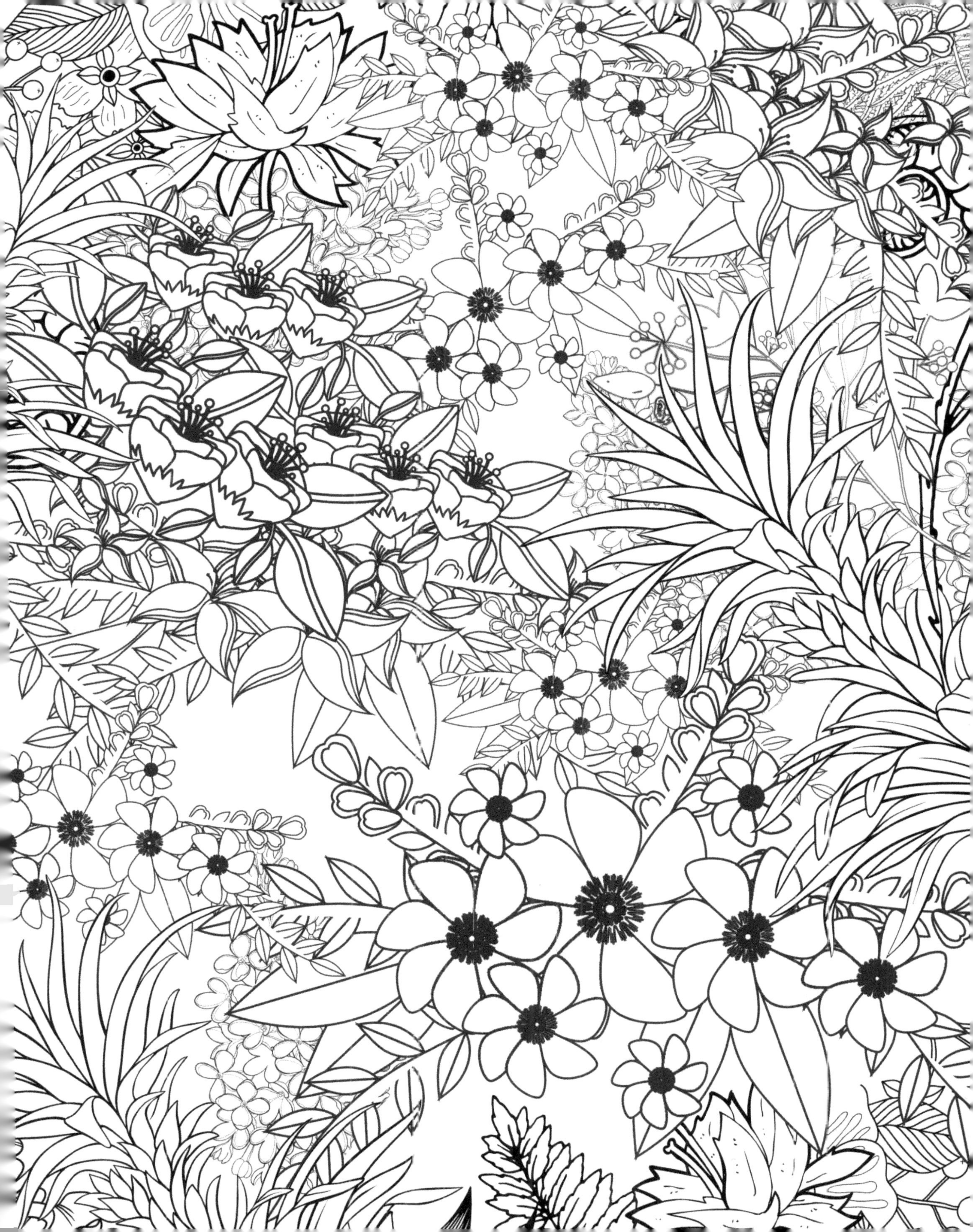

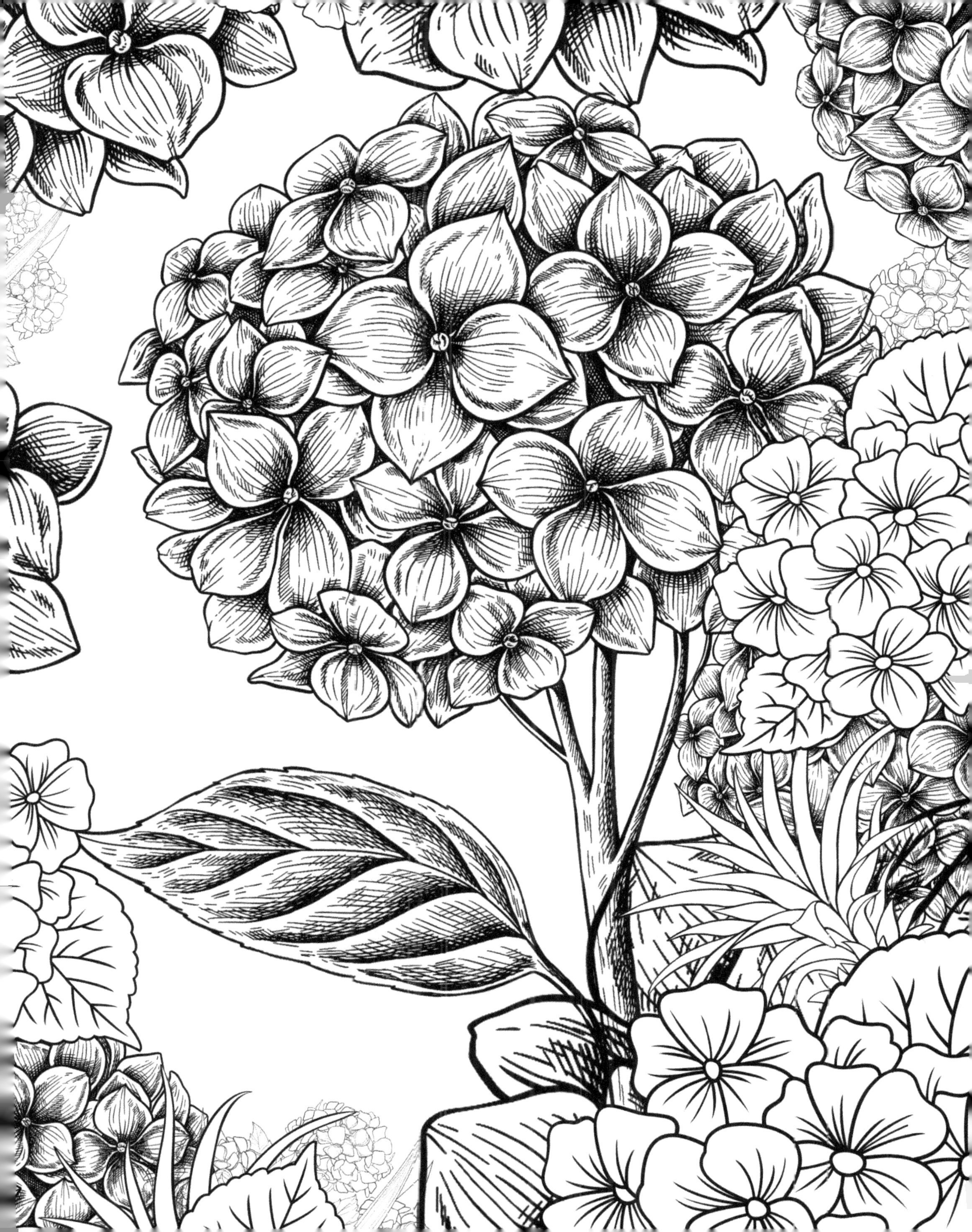

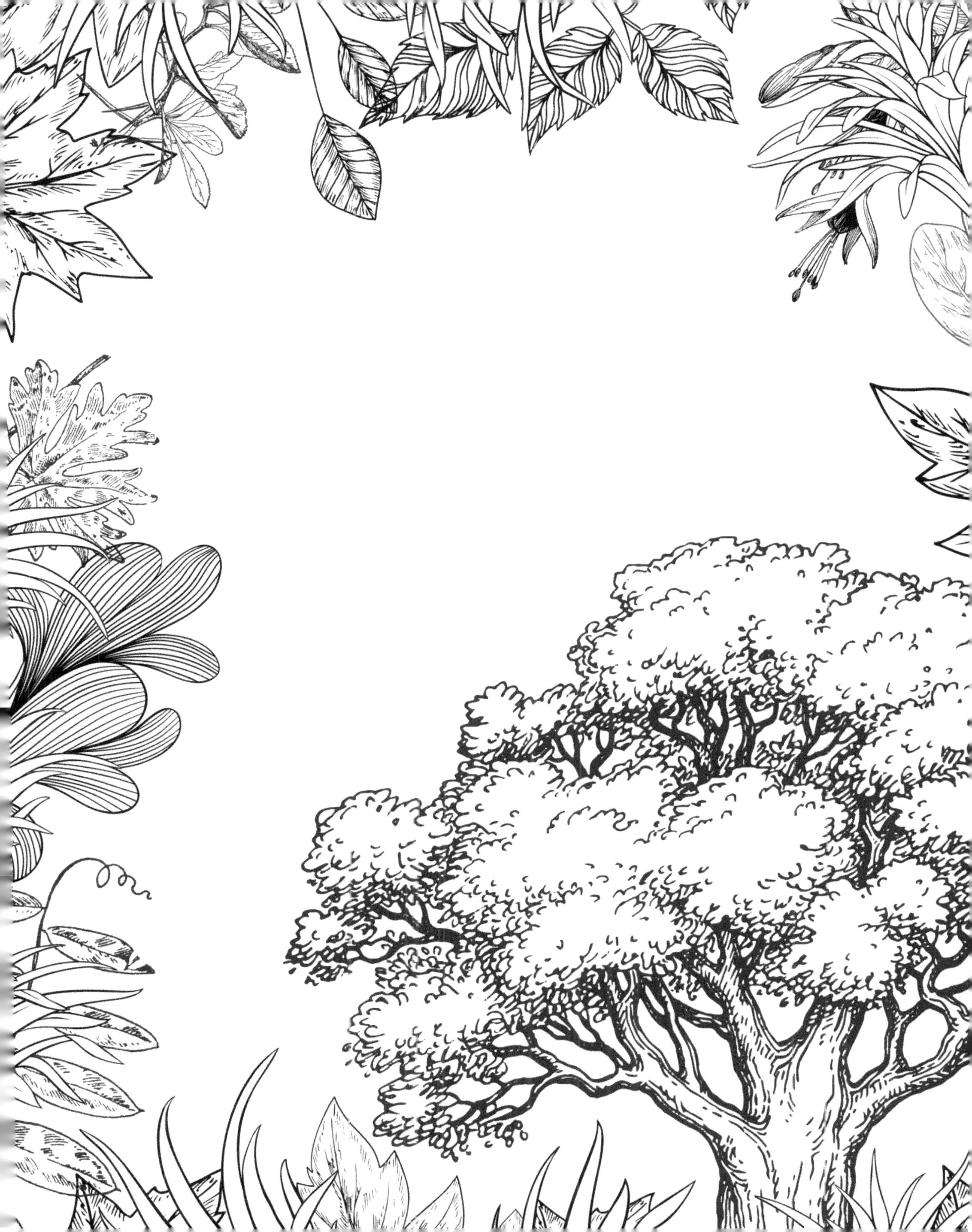

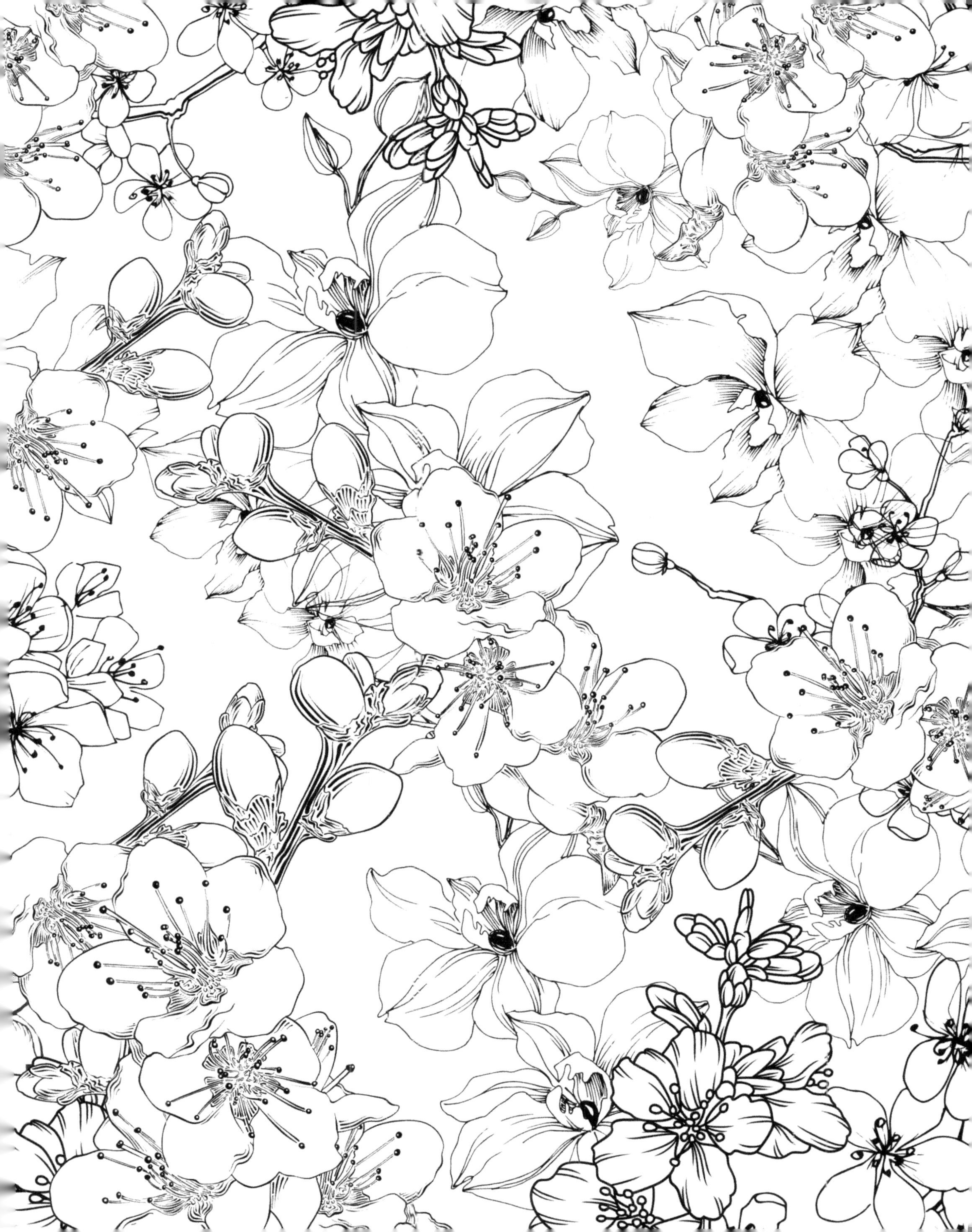

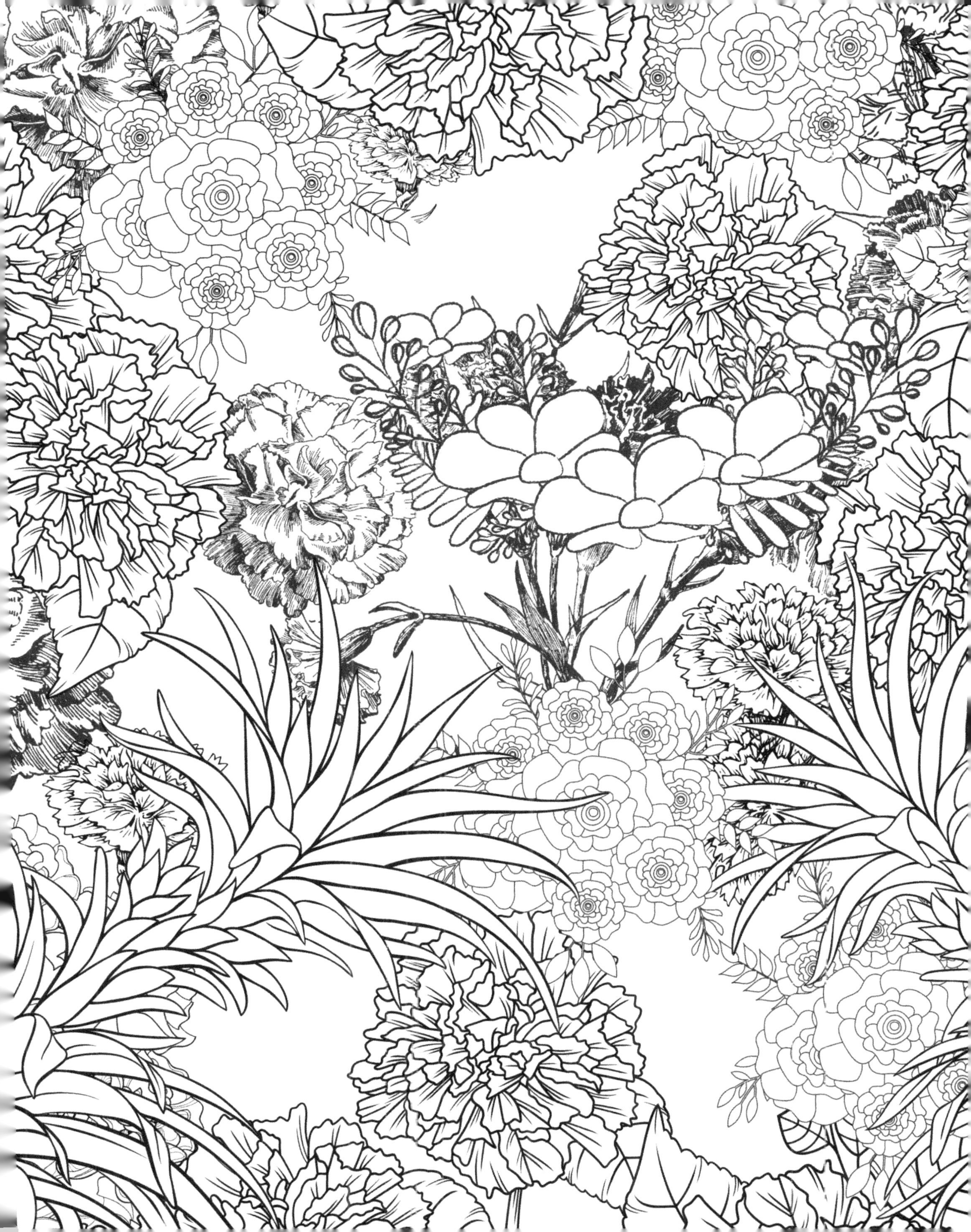

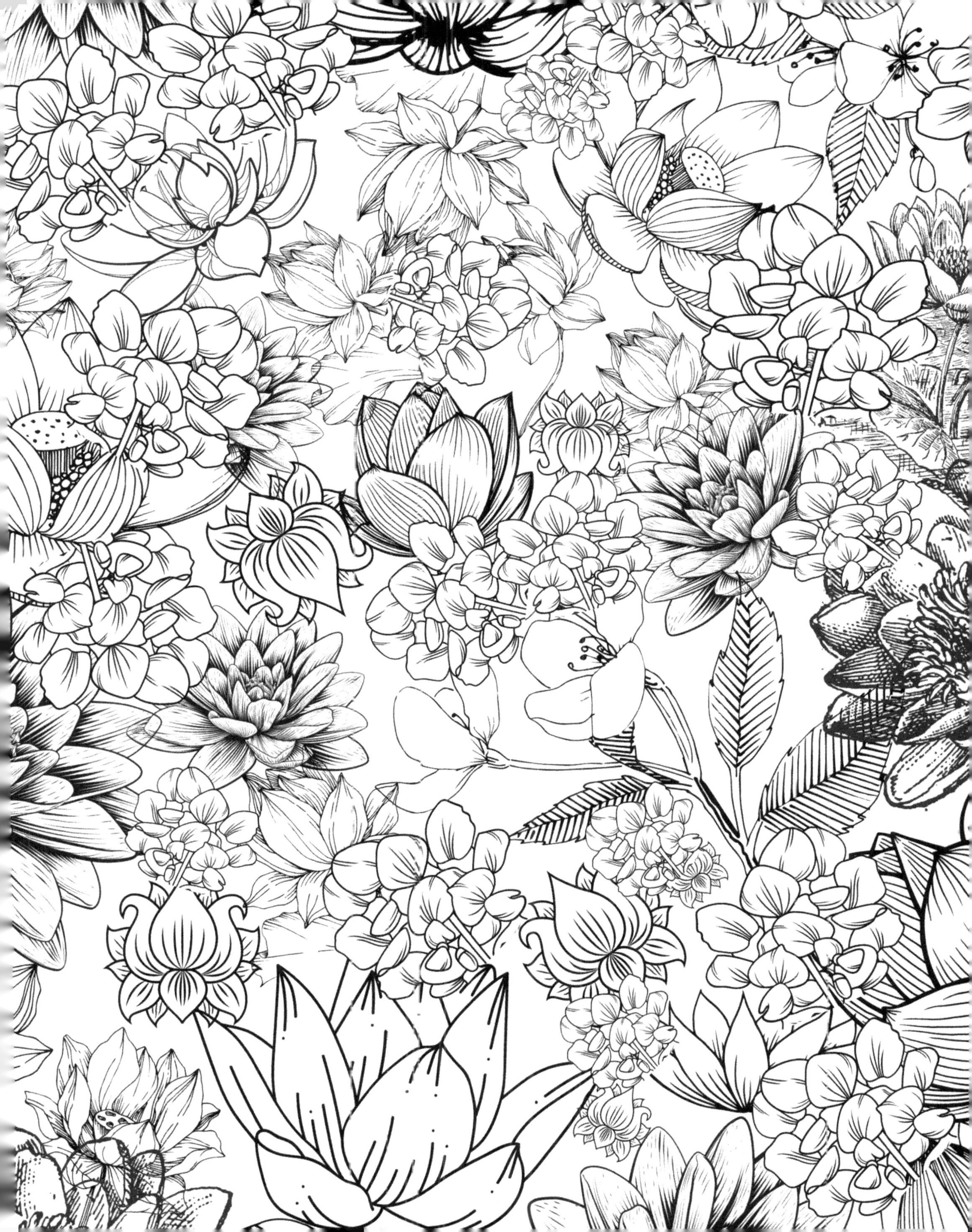

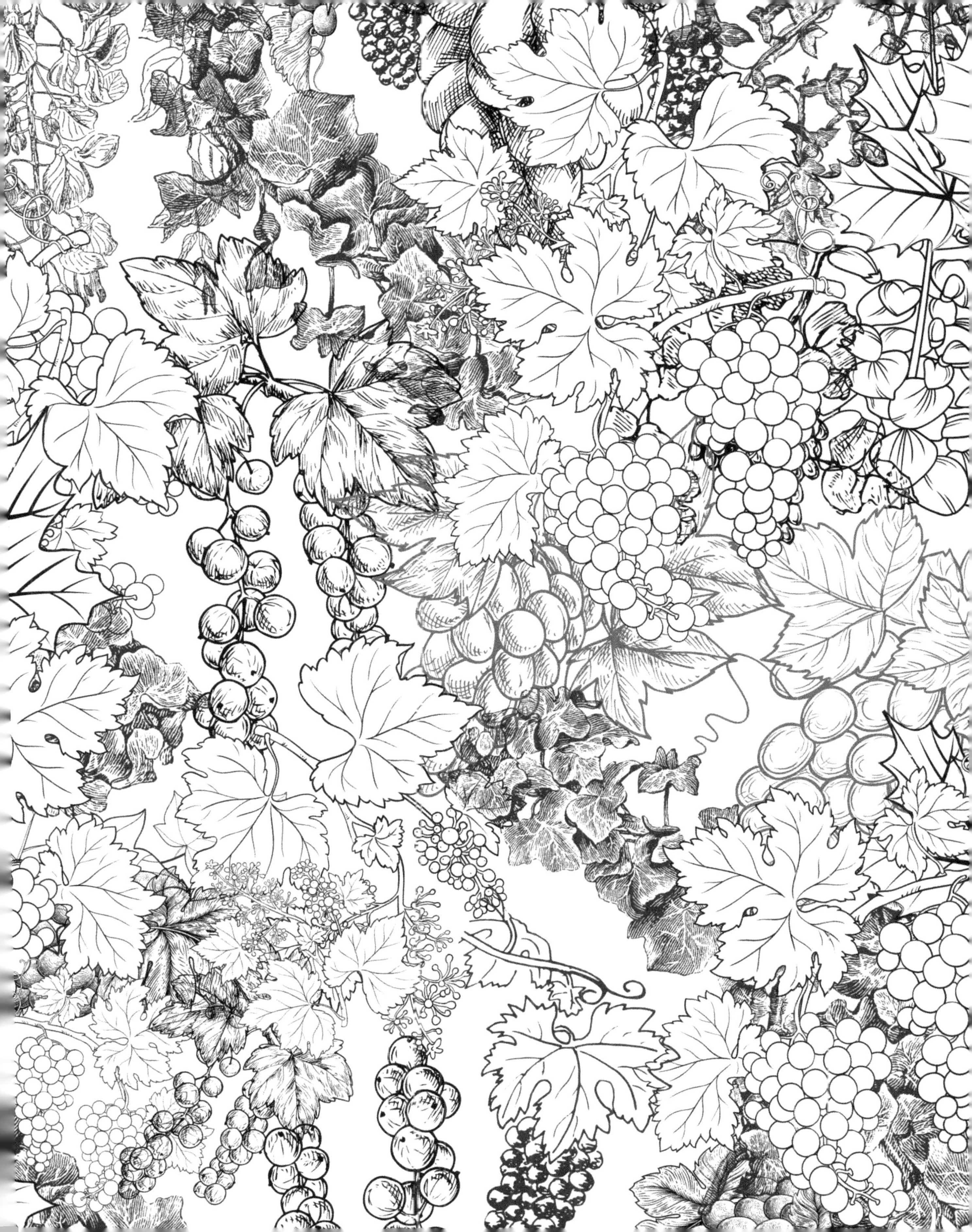

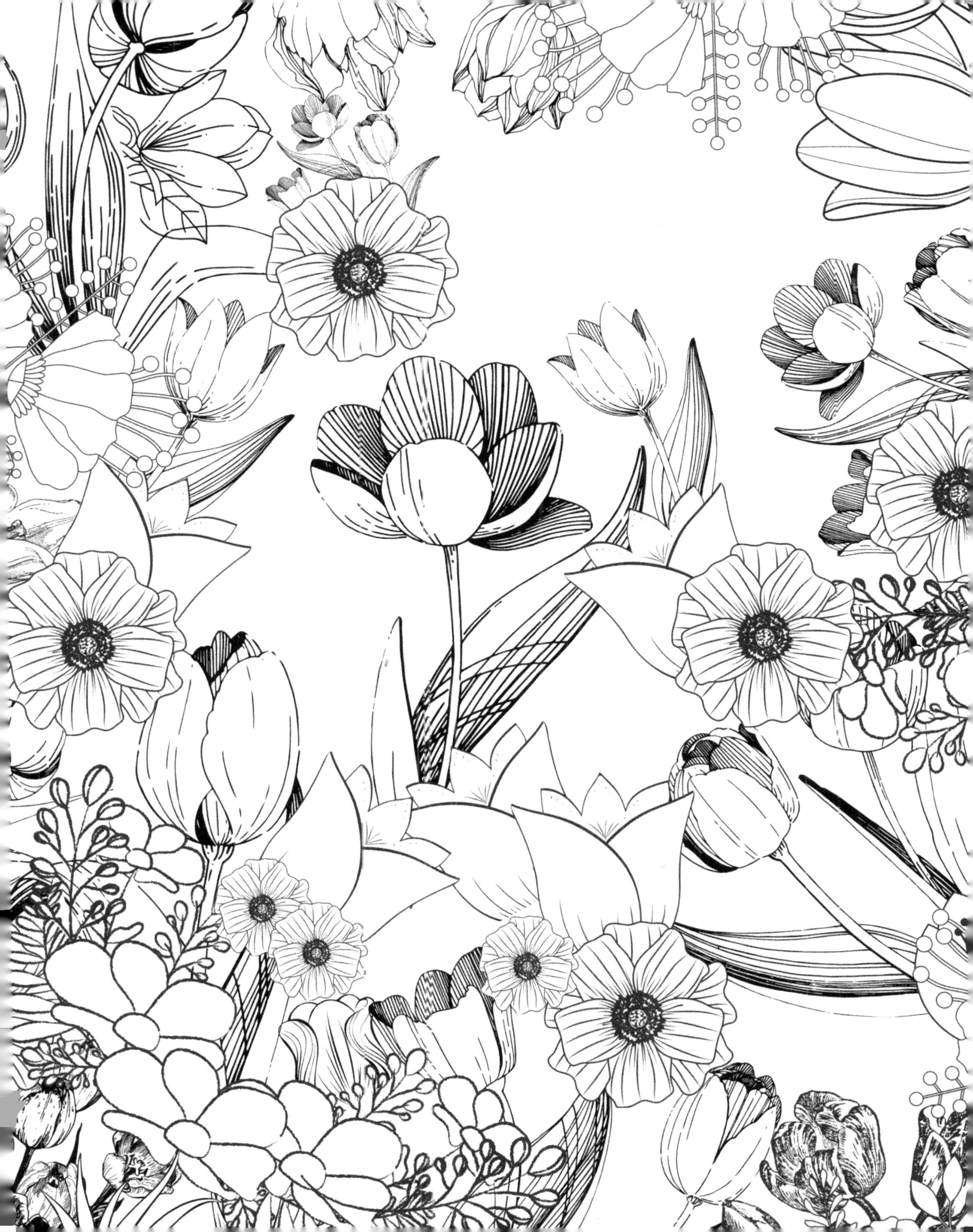

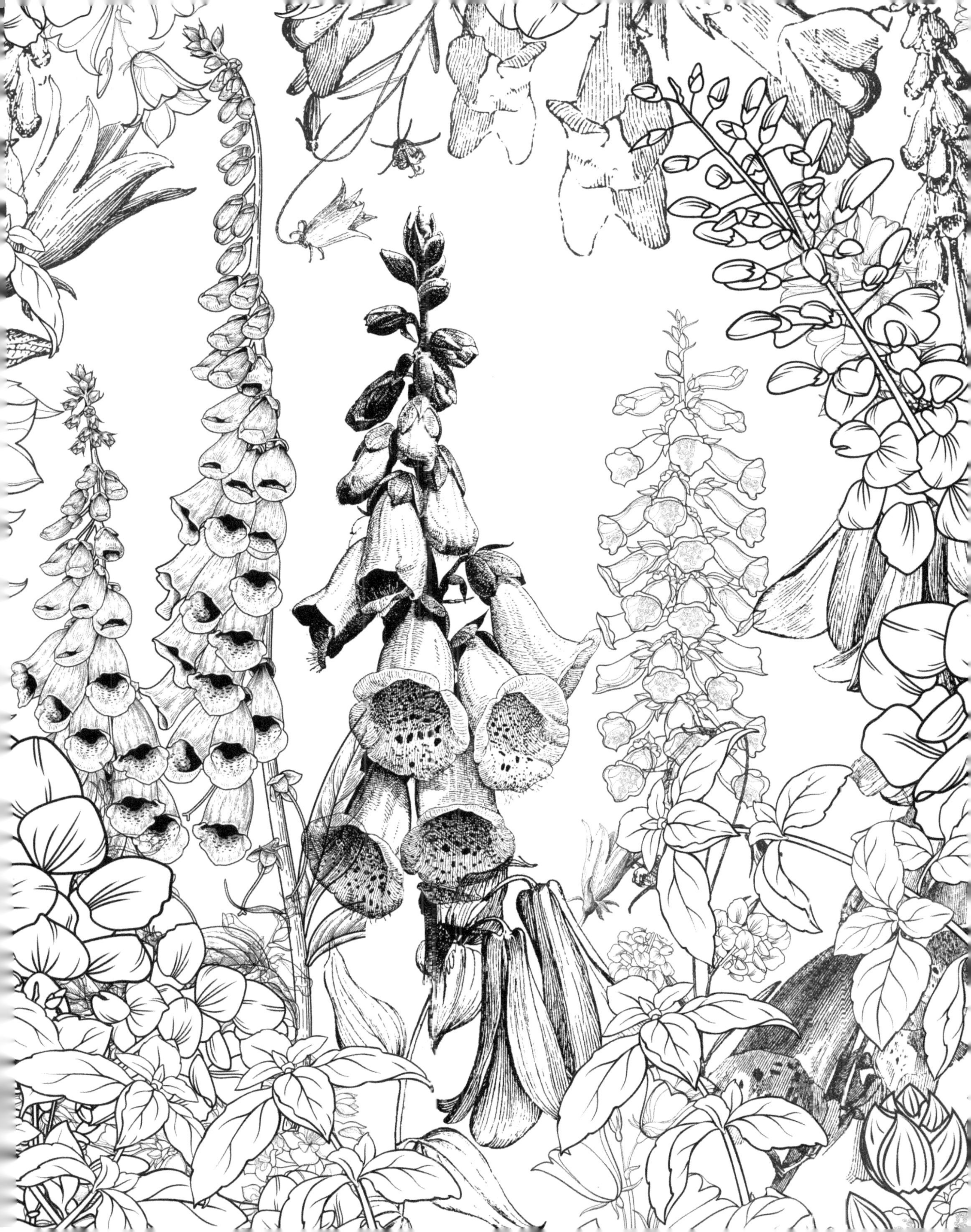

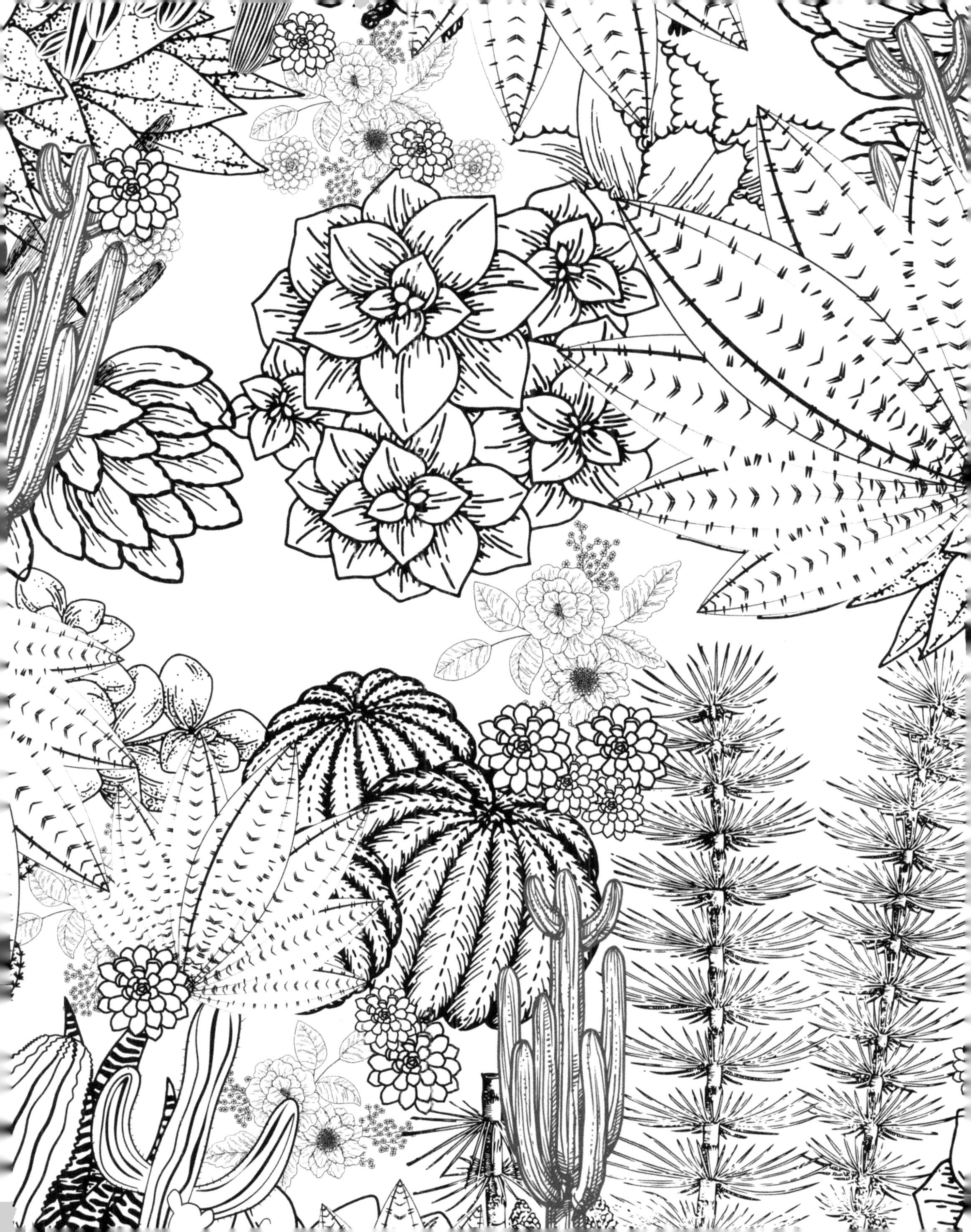

www.ingramcontent.com/pod-product-compliance
Lightning Source LLC
Chambersburg PA
CBHW081652270326
41933CB00018B/3443